ALL YOU NEED IS A GOAL

The 5-Step Plan to Get Rid of Regret and Unlock Your Massive Potential

By

Ricky A. Bergman

Contents

INTRODUCTION

Regret is a powerful feeling that may haunt you, reminding you of squandered opportunities and the roads not chosen. It might leave you stuck and unfulfilled, wondering what could have been. But what if there was a way to break free from regret? What if there was a simple 5-step method that might help you unlock your vast potential and live a life without regrets?

It all starts with a goal. Having a clear vision of what you desire is the first step toward breaking free from regret. When you have a plan in mind, whether starting a business, pursuing a hobby, or improving your health, you give yourself something to strive for. It creates a fire within you, propelling you ahead and giving you a sense of purpose.

But setting a goal is just the beginning. The next stage is breaking it down into doable jobs. By dividing your goal into more miniature, manageable stages, you make it less overwhelming and more accessible. Each step completed brings you closer to your intended objective, creating momentum and confidence along the way.

Taking action is vital, especially in the face of dread and doubt. It's natural to feel scared when going into the unknown, but it's crucial to remember that growth and progress lie outside your comfort zone. By embracing the discomfort and taking that first step, you open yourself to new possibilities and chances.

Setbacks and setbacks are unavoidable, but they should never be considered as reasons to give up. Instead, they should be regarded as great lessons and opportunities for progress. Learning from your mistakes and using them as stepping stones towards your goal differentiates those who achieve from those who remain stuck in regret.

Persistence and adaptation are crucial. The journey toward your goal may sometimes be complicated, and you may encounter barriers. But by sticking with determination and modifying your approach as necessary, you can overcome any problem that comes your way.

In this 5-step approach, we'll explore how setting goals, breaking them down into achievable tasks, taking action despite fear and doubt, learning from setbacks, and persisting with flexibility can help you live without regret and unlock your vast potential. So, let's go on this trip together and discover the great possibilities that await you when you have a goal and the confidence to achieve it.

WHY YOU NEED TO SET A GOAL

It is hard to overstate the benefits of setting a goal. Setting a goal may do many things for you: direction, focus, and even create chances. It can take you to a different planet, physically and emotionally. Here are some factors to keep in mind when creating a goal:

1. Measuring Progress and Achievement

Goals provide a measurable approach to track your progress and recognize your achievements. By creating specified, measurable, achievable, relevant, and time-bound (SMART) goals, you develop a framework to analyze your advancement. Regularly examining your progress allows you to recognize how far you've gone and find areas for growth. It delivers a sense of satisfaction and fulfillment when you hit milestones and accomplish what you set out to do, improving your self-confidence and self-belief.

2. Direction and Clarity

Goals provide you with direction and clarity in life. They help you prioritize your time and resources, ensuring that you're working toward what matters most to you. With goals, it's easier to become aimless and clear about where you're headed. Setting objectives helps you chart a route and make educated decisions, leading to a more purposeful and fulfilling existence.

3. Motivation and Focus

Setting clear and detailed goals provides motivation and focus. When you have a stated objective, you're more likely to stay engaged and work regularly toward accomplishing it. Plans offer you a cause to wake up with passion and purpose. Whether it's a personal goal like improving your health or a professional objective like growing in your career, having a plan may fuel your efforts and help you concentrate on what truly counts.

<u>1</u>

PERSONAL DEVELOPMENT JOURNEYS

"The path to success is to take massive, determined action."- Anthony Robbins

A personal development journey is the pursuit of self-improvement and advancement in areas such as career, relationships, health, and emotional well-being. It entails setting meaningful goals, learning new abilities, and increasing self-awareness. These life-changing experiences necessitate self-reflection, dedication, and stepping outside one's comfort zone. Personal growth improves overall well-being, boosts self-confidence, and encourages resilience. It is a lifetime pursuit that is unique to each individual and is motivated by a desire to attain their full potential and live a more fulfilling life via continual learning, self-discovery, and embracing growth chances. Spending time with people who want to develop themselves can also benefit you, and here are a few things you will notice they:

Set clear and achievable goals

Many people who have experienced great personal improvement credit this strategy. By forming well-defined objectives, they acquired a profound feeling of purpose and direction. These objectives served as a guide map for their personal improvement journey, sparking their passion for constant enhancement. With every milestone accomplished, their self-assurance and belief in their talents soared, propelling them toward being the finest version of themselves. Ultimately, creating clear and attainable goals is a shared quality among people who have achieved tremendous leaps in their personal growth, affording them attention, incentives, and a tangible pathway to self-improvement.

Learn continuously

Dr. Theodor Seuss wrote, *"The more that you read, the more things you will know. The more that you learn the more places you'll go."*

Continuous learning is a potent stimulant for personal development, and countless individuals who have dramatically improved their personal development attribute their commitment to this discipline. By embracing a philosophy of continual education, they've expanded their knowledge and refined new abilities, enabling them to adapt to changing circumstances and embrace fresh possibilities. This drive to learn has not only extended their perspectives but also increased their problem-solving ability and confidence. It's a common thread among people who have transformed themselves, indicating that a commitment to lifelong learning can lead to tremendous personal development and growth.

Practice self-reflection

The habit of self-reflection is a common thread among persons who have successfully boosted their personal development. Many attribute their improvement to this vital practice, stressing how routinely taking time to introspect and assess their experiences, decisions, and emotions has provided valuable insights into their actions and thought processes. This self-awareness forms the cornerstone for positive transformation, helping them to recognize areas for growth, establish meaningful goals, and make well-informed decisions. Through constant self-reflection, these individuals have gained self-esteem, emotional intelligence, and general personal development, leading to more meaningful and purposeful lives.

Prioritize self-care

Prioritizing self-care is a critical component of personal growth for people who have achieved major life gains. These individuals know that taking care of their physical, mental, and emotional well-being is the foundation upon which personal progress is based. By committing time to self-care, people refresh themselves, manage stress more effectively, and retain a happy outlook. This practice helps them to confront obstacles with resilience and confidence, ultimately leading to a more balanced, full, and successful life.

Seek feedback and support from others

Actively seeking feedback and assistance from others stands out as a significant feature contributing to the personal development achievement of several individuals. Individuals who have achieved major strides in their improvement owe their advancement to this practice. Through their proactive attempts to seek input from trusted mentors, coaches, friends, and colleagues, they acquire vital perspectives and insights that enable them to spot areas for improvement and uncover fresh pathways for progress. This feedback not only allows people to question their preconceptions, extend their perspectives, and make more informed judgments but also builds a network of encouragement, accountability, and direction. This network serves as a vital resource during hard times, facilitating the development of new knowledge and abilities, as well as receiving constructive criticism to fine-tune their goals and tactics. Ultimately, seeking external feedback and encouragement plays a key part in personal growth, encouraging individuals to learn, grow, and realize their full potential. It cultivates a dynamic environment that bolsters self-improvement and prepares individuals to handle difficulties with heightened confidence and efficacy.

2

GOAL SETTING STRATEGIES

"A goal without a plan is just a wish."
- Antoine de Saint-Exupéry

Goal-setting strategies are the guidebook to bringing fantasies into reality. These tactics involve creating defined, achievable, and time-bound objectives. The SMART (Specific, Measurable, Achievable, Relevant, Time-bound) principles are a foundation for effective goal setting. Additionally, dividing larger goals into smaller, manageable steps makes the process less frightening and more feasible. Consistency, constant evaluation, and adaptation are key factors to achieve growth. Goal-setting tactics not only provide focus but also empower individuals to overcome hurdles, quantify accomplishments, and turn dreams into tangible achievements. There are numerous goal-setting strategies, but some of the most effective are as follows:

Use goal-setting frameworks

Goal-setting frameworks are structured systems that provide a systematic manner to identify, plan, and attain objectives. They help people, teams, and organizations set clear and achievable goals, track progress, and stay motivated. Here are several popular goal-setting frameworks: SMART (Specific, Measurable, Achievable, Relevant, and Time-bound) Framework, OKRs

(Objectives and Key Results) Framework, B.H.A.G. (Big, Hairy, Audacious Goals) Framework, FAST (Frequently discussed, Ambitious, Specific, and Transparent) Framework. No matter the framework you use, the objective is to identify a goal-setting technique that works for you and your organization's specific needs. By using these frameworks, you may develop effective goals that help you achieve success in your personal and professional life.

Break down goals into smaller steps

Goals can be made more manageable and less intimidating by breaking them down into smaller steps. It is one of the most crucial goal-setting techniques. You may make your goals more feasible and less intimidating by breaking them down into smaller steps. This method can assist you in remaining focused, motivated, and on track to meet your goals. Begin by determining the main aim you wish to attain when breaking down your goals. This should be a high-level goal that includes the key objectives you aim to attain. Once you've determined your major aim, divide it into smaller, more doable phases. Specific, quantifiable, realistic, relevant, and time-bound steps should be taken. Then, rank the steps you've identified regarding priority and urgency. This will allow you to prioritize the most important things—set deadlines for each phase to help you stay focused and motivated. Check if the timelines are reasonable and doable, in addition to routinely monitoring your progress and adjusting your approach as needed. To keep motivated, celebrate your victories along the road. This strategy not only boosts motivation but also provides a clear path to the ultimate goal. It's a tried-and-true method for turning lofty goals into manageable steps.

Creating a plan of action

Creating a plan of action is an important step toward accomplishing your objectives. It entails detailing the particular procedures and tactics needed to achieve your goals. This strategy will serve as a road map to guide your efforts and keep you on track. It assists you in remaining organized, effectively managing your time, and allocating resources. You can boost your chances of achieving your goals by developing a plan of action. Here are some pointers for developing an effective action plan:

- Make your objectives explicit and quantifiable.
- Divide your objectives into smaller, more doable activities.
- Set deadlines for each task and prioritize them.
- Determine the resources required to execute each task.
- Assign tasks to others and keep track of your progress.

Creating a plan of action may be a lot of work, but it will be worth it. You are more likely to attain your goals if you take the time to plan them.

Tracking your progress

Tracking your progress is an essential element of achieving your goals. It entails regularly monitoring and analyzing your actions and results in connection to your goals. This technique not only holds you accountable, but it also assists you in identifying areas where your approach may need to be adjusted. You could keep a journal or log to track your development on a regular basis. Examine your outcomes on a regular and critical basis to discover your strengths, weaknesses, opportunities, and threats and to inform your next steps. Here are some more pointers for tracking your progress:

- Make use of a visual system. Visually tracking your development might be more motivating and helpful.
- Celebrate your accomplishments. It is critical to recognize and appreciate your accomplishments along the journey. This will keep you motivated and going forward.
- Don't be frightened to make changes. If you're not making progress, don't be scared to change your strategy. This could include altering your goals, breaking them down into smaller steps, or establishing new deadlines.

<u>3</u>

<u>**OVERCOMING REGRET**</u>

"Remorse is the poison of life."

- Charlotte Bronte

Regret is a common human emotion. It happens to everyone from time to time. However, if regret is not handled properly, it can have a severe impact on our lives. Recognizing your feelings and accepting what has occurred is the first step toward overcoming regret. Allow yourself to be forgiven and learn from your mistakes. Regret can be a beneficial learning experience. Take some time to think about what went wrong and how you can prevent making the same mistake again. Focus on the present as well, and make the most of every chance.

Overcoming regrets can be a little overwhelming, so here are a few tips on how to deal with regret:

Let yourself feel regret

Regret is a natural sensation that can be tough to deal with. However, allowing yourself to feel remorse is a vital step in the process of healing and personal growth. It's about admitting the emotions related to prior choices or acts, rather than ignoring or rejecting them. By allowing oneself permission to feel remorse, you open the door to self-reflection and understanding. This emotional awareness can be a catalyst for transformation, pushing you to learn from your mistakes, make reparations when necessary, and ultimately move forward with greater wisdom and resilience. It's a key aspect of the journey towards self-forgiveness and personal development. To deal with regret, it's necessary to put it into perspective, learn from it, build self-compassion and forgiveness, and seek support. By utilizing these tactics, you can learn to deal with regret and change it into a positive force in your life.

Put your regrets into perspective

Placing your regrets in context is a vital component of resolving them effectively. Regret possesses the potential to be a tremendous and paralyzing force, often creating worry and anxiety. Nevertheless, by reframing your viewpoint, you can transform remorse into a positive learning experience. Recognizing that remorse is a universal sense shared by all individuals can be freeing. Rather than obsessing over its negative features, it can function as a guiding compass to disclose your true objectives and aspirations.

Furthermore, modifying your view of regret is feasible through introspection, communicating your sentiments with a trusted confidant, using them to match your ideals, and leveraging them as an instructional tool. Employing these tactics promotes a constructive approach to dealing with regrets, turning their energy into positive personal growth and resilience.

Cultivate self-compassion and forgiveness

Cultivating self-compassion and forgiveness is a transforming path that can lead to deep human improvement. It means treating yourself with kindness, understanding, and acceptance, especially in the face of mistakes, failures, and shortcomings. Practicing self-compassion and self-forgiveness can be challenging, particularly if you have a history of self-criticism or have endured trauma or painful life situations. However, there are various techniques that can help you build these vital qualities.

These include being compassionate to oneself, acknowledging your common humanity, and maintaining a balanced perspective on your feelings and experiences. Self-compassion helps you avoid self-criticism and negative self-talk, which can be destructive to your mental health and well-being. When you practice self-compassion, you learn to embrace yourself, flaws and all, and to treat yourself with the same level of kindness and care that you would offer to a loved one. Forgiveness, both of yourself and, where applicable, others, is a critical component of this process. It doesn't mean condoning past actions; rather, it's about releasing the grip of resentment and negative feelings. By practicing self-compassion and forgiveness, you can learn to deal with regret and transform it into a good force in your life.

Here are some other suggestions for dealing with regrets:

- Speak with someone you trust who can assist you in processing your regrets and developing a plan for moving forward.
- Be gentle with yourself and recognize that everyone makes errors.
- Concentrate on your strengths and accomplishments.
- Set new goals to work towards, concentrate on the future, and let go of your regrets.

4

Unlocking Your Potential

"Our potential lies between what is and what could be." - Kim Butler

Unlocking your potential is a lifetime endeavor that requires self-examination, goal-setting, and self-discipline. To unlock your fullest potential, you must put yourself under a microscope and look at some essential areas with a critical eye. You need the aid of others, as they can be mentors, coaches, and resources for you while you navigate unfamiliar ground. To unleash your potential, you must have goals that give direction for your energy and work. You must also dream large, start small, and create excellent habits. Embracing challenges, focusing on effort over outcome, and having a sense that you can grow and improve are essential components of realizing your maximum potential. By following these principles, you may unlock your potential and attain your goals.

When seeking to unlock your potential, you should consider:

Get to know yourself

Getting to know oneself is a vital step in unlocking your potential. Self-awareness is the foundation of personal growth and development. It helps you understand your strengths, limitations, values, and beliefs. Self-awareness also helps you find areas for growth and set goals that match your values and aspirations. To get to know yourself, you can practice mindfulness, reflect on your experiences, and seek input from others. You can also take personality tests, journal, and engage in self-reflection. By getting to know yourself, you may unlock your potential and achieve your goals. Remember that self-awareness is a lifetime path, and it involves continual work and self-reflection.

Challenge yourself

Challenge yourself is a call to venture out of your comfort zone and push your limitations. It's a tremendous stimulus for personal growth and development. By establishing ambitious goals and facing new and unusual experiences, you might find your hidden potential, develop new abilities, and build resilience. Challenges create possibilities for learning and self-discovery. They test your abilities and extend your horizons, leading to enhanced confidence and a deeper awareness of your potential. Embracing challenges may lead to extraordinary achievements and a more rewarding life as you break through self-imposed limitations and push for new heights. It's a mindset that motivates you toward ongoing self-improvement and the attainment of your full potential.

Be persistent

Being persistent is a critical step in uncovering your potential. It entails taking constant action towards your goals, even when faced with hurdles or disappointments. Persistence helps you develop resilience, determination, and a positive attitude. To be persistent, you must have a strong desire to attain your goals, and you must be prepared to put in the effort required to reach them. You can foster persistence by creating reasonable goals, breaking them down into smaller steps, and praising your accomplishments along the way. You can also seek assistance from others, exercise self-care, and have a growth mentality. Remember that persistence is a journey, and it involves continual work and self-reflection. By investing in yourself and your personal growth, you may unlock your full potential and achieve your goals.

Surround yourself with positive people

Surrounding yourself with positive people is one of the best things you can do for your physical and mental wellbeing. Positive people can help you stay motivated, focused, and optimistic. They can also provide you with support and encouragement when you need it most. Positive individuals can also inspire you, help you become successful, and urge you not to stop when you find yourself in a difficult circumstance.

Positive people offer not just encouragement but also constructive comments, establishing a sense of community that encourages personal progress. Surrounding yourself with positive individuals is a vital aspect of living a happy and fulfilling life. Remember, you are the average of the five people you spend the most time with, so choose wisely.

5

SUCCESS STORIES

"He Who is Not Courageous Enough to Take Risks Will Accomplish Nothing in Life" - Muhammad Ali

Success stories are inspiring accounts of individuals or organizations who have achieved their goals despite encountering challenges and hurdles. These stories can motivate and inspire others to pursue their dreams and unlock their potential. Success tales can be found in different industries, including business, sports, education, and personal growth. They generally involve individuals who have overcome hardship, persevered through difficult circumstances, and attained their goals through hard work, tenacity, and resilience. Success stories can provide significant insights into the techniques and tactics that successful people employ to achieve their goals. They can also help individuals learn from the experiences of others and apply those lessons to their own lives. Whether you are looking for inspiration or assistance, success stories can be a helpful resource for unleashing your potential and achieving your goals.

Some of the crucial factors to take attention to in a success story are:

- A clear goal or objective. What did the person wish to achieve?
- Obstacles or difficulties. What did the person have to overcome in order to reach their goal

- Action steps. What did the person do to achieve their goal?
- Results. What did the person gain as a result of their efforts?
- Lessons learned. What did the person learn from their experience that can be useful to others?

ALL YOU NEED IS A GOAL

ONE LAST THOUGHT

I hope you enjoyed this book. As you move on, I wish you success and recommend that you keep in mind:

1. "Without goals, and plans to reach them, you are like a ship that has set sail with no destination." — Fitzhugh Dodson

2. "People with goals succeed because they know where they're going." — Earl Nightingale

3. "A year from now you may wish you had started today." — Karen Lamb

4. "If a goal is worth having, it's worth blocking out the time in your day-to-day life necessary to achieve it." — Jill Koenig

5. "Life is not easy for any of us. But what of that? We must have perseverance and above all confidence in ourselves. We must believe that we are gifted for something and that this thing must be attained." — Marie Curie